MEL BAY'S
EASY BANJO
SOLOS

by
Dick Weissman

Here are some new pieces for banjo that can be played by a student who knows the basic chords in the G tuning. I have presented a variety of musical styles and banjo techniques, including hammering on, pulling off, string-bending and slides. I have included chords for the pieces so that a guitarist or another banjoist can play along. All of these solos use up-picking in the right hand, except the three frailing pieces on pages 27–29. Play the up-picking pieces with fingerpicks and they will gradually ease you into bluegrass.

— Dick Weissman

BOOK and CD CONTENTS

1 2 3 4 5 6 7 8 9 0

Visit us on the Web at http://www.melbay.com
E-mail us at email@melbay.com

Thumbs First

This entire piece is played by the thumb and first finger of the right hand. It can be played with or without the use of fingerpicks. The only chord is G, which requires no left-hand fingerings. I have marked the right-hand fingering. "T" means Thumb; "1" means index finger.

Indexed

Here is another piece that uses only the G chord, and the thumb and index fingers of the right hand. If you start playing with fingerpicks now, you will be prepared for later pieces in the bluegrass style. I have marked the right-hand fingerings.

Two-Finger Waltz

The right-hand fingering here varies: sometimes it uses thumb and first finger, sometimes thumb, first and second finger. Be sure to notice that this tune is in 3/4 time. There are three beats in each measure.

2+T

Another piece for the thumb and two fingers. Notice the D7 chord on line two. The symbol C at he beginning of the piece means common time, which is 4/4 time.

T+2

Be careful to observe the right-hand fingering. I have deliberately varied the picking, so that sometimes the first finger picks consecutive notes, while at other times the first and second fingers alternate.

Music Bar Rag

The right-hand fingering pattern in this tune usually alternates between the thumb and first finger. You can also try it with the thumb playing the fifth string only, and the first and second fingers alternating on the other strings.

6/8 Irish

6/8 time is counted <u>1</u> 2 3 <u>4</u> 5 6 with the accents on 1 and 4. If you are tapping your feet, tap two beats to the measure and silently count all six beats.

Three-Chord Tune

This melody introduces the C chord, which uses three fingers of the left hand.

Little Hammers

In hammering on, a note is produced by the left-hand fretting the strings. Play the first note of this piece on the open third string then, with the middle finger of the left hand, fret the third string at the second fret without picking it. All the hammer notes are marked with an "H."

If you are not getting any notes with your hammering on, one of two things is happening. If you are hammering on too quickly you will lose the first note; if you wait too long you will not get the second note. Keep your rhythm even.

You Have a Hammer

Another study in hammering on. Keep the notes even.

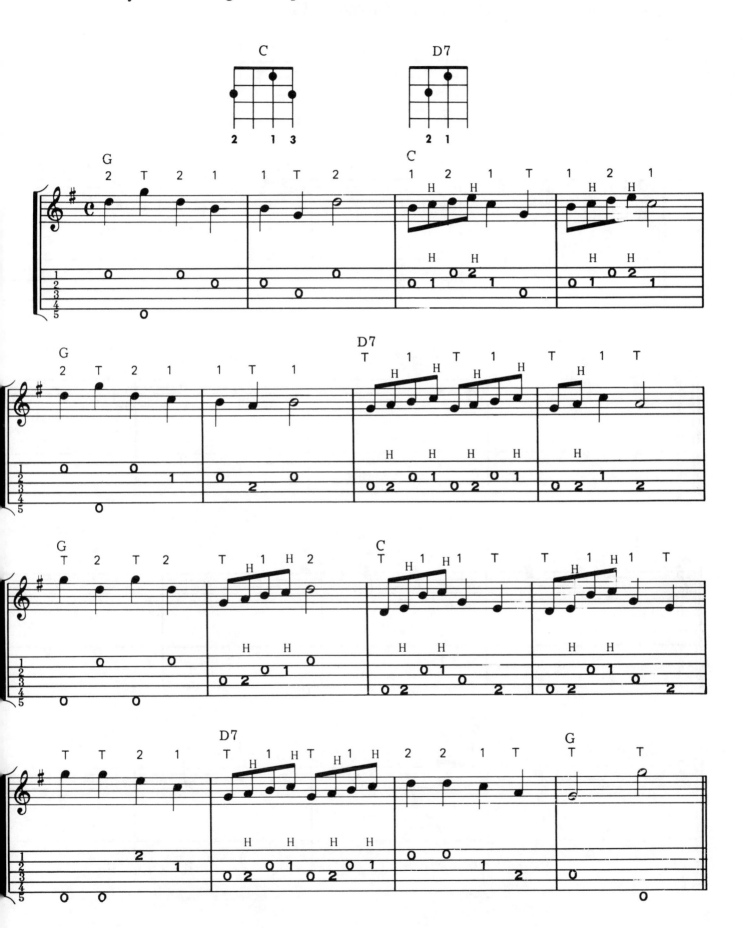

Hammer 'n Pinch

A pinch describes what happens when two notes are played together. It is a technique used in bluegrass to play rhythm, instead of playing full chords. This piece is in 3/4 time.

G Hammers

This tune includes quite a few hammers that require you to finger strings with the open G chord. These notes are not in the chord, but sound good because they are neighbor notes to notes in that chord.

Different Hammers

It is possible to hammer on a different string than the one you are picking with the right hand. In this solo the first note is the right-hand middle finger picking the open first string, and the second note is produced with a left-hand hammer at the third string, second fret. Once you get used to this technique you will find it greatly expands the potential uses of hammering on.

Pulling

In pulling off, the left hand pulls the string off the fingerboard. The third note of this piece is produced this way, by the pull-off at the first string, second fret. Pull-offs are marked with a "P."

Double Pulls

Watch out for the double pulls on the second and third lines, where two fingers are pulling off at the same time. Notice that this piece has 13 bars instead of the usual 12 or 16 bars.

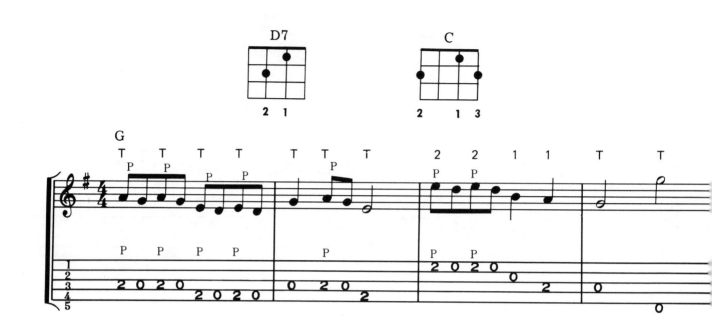

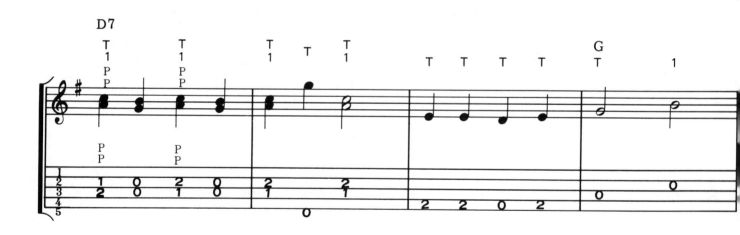

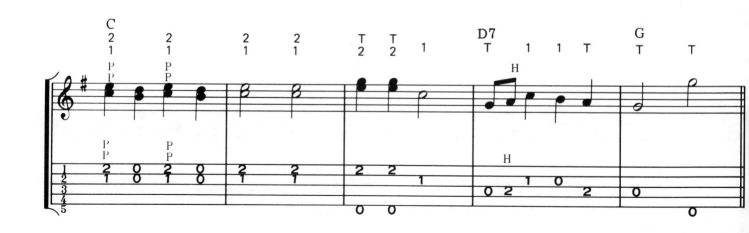

Blues Bends

To play "Blues Bends," stretch each string marked with a "B." This will raise the pitch of the note. This technique is often used in blues and rock guitar playing.

Using Pull

This piece uses hammers, pull-offs and bends. The very last half note is an open G chord. To play it brush down with the first or second finger of the right hand.

Pulling Waltz

This piece uses pull-offs where one finger is pulling off while another note is held. This device is found in the second note of the piece. I have written the "P" adjacent to the string because of the held note.

Slidin'

To play a slide, first pick the note with the right hand, then the left-hand finger slides to the proper fret. Check the tablature to find the correct fret.

Irish Breakfast

Another Irish-flavored tune in 6/8. Remember to count 2 beats to the bar, 1 2 3 4 5 6. Try this one without picks. This solo uses the F chord, which is diagrammed below. The D notes in the sixth and tenth bars are played on the second string (third fret).

Slowin' Earl Down

A simple bluegrass tune. I have written the rhythm in groups of 3 + 3 + 2 eighth notes, rather than groups of 4 eighths, because the accents should fall on the first, fourth and seventh notes. Be sure to use your picks on this one.

Mostly Thumbs

"Mostly Thumbs" is a bluegrass pattern where the thumb plays most of the leads. This is a useful pattern, and requires finger flexibility, because the order of right-hand fingers is thumb, first, second, thumb, second, first, thumb, first finger.

24

Exterior Fog

This tune uses the same chord progression as the famous Scruggs tune, "Foggy Mountain Breakdown." The E minor chord is diagrammed below.

Mixin' It Up

The finger that starts each roll (group of 8 eighth notes) is called the "lead finger." This tune constantly shifts the lead finger, and will require a bit of practice.

26

Fret Not, Frail Some

Frailing is executed with the index finger picking down on the single notes. Some people use the second finger of the right hand, but I prefer the first finger. Try it both ways. Brush strokes are played by the second finger. Keep your wrist relaxed, and be patient.

Pickin' Down

Another frailing tune. The second finger strums all chords or double notes. Don't be surprised if you aim at one string but hit another one for the first few weeks that you try to frail.

Mountain Water

For the last frailing tune I have used the chord change G to F, a common one in the music of the Southern mountains. Once again remember to pick all single notes with the first finger, except for the fifth string, which is played by the thumb.

Something in C

The last three tunes in this book are in the C tuning. Tune your fourth string down from D to C. This note is an octave lower than the second string fingered at the first fret. The correct chord diagrams are printed below, and I have given the right-hand fingerings. In this tune the right hand returns to up-picking (bluegrass) style. Use your picks.

Something Else in C

Another solo to give you more practice in the C tuning.

Major Minor

You will need to learn the C minor chord, diagrammed below, to play this solo.